Chapter 1: Introduction to APIs

What is an API?

In the world of technology, the term "API" stands for Application Programming Interface. But what exactly does that mean? At its core, an API is a set of rules and protocols that allows different software applications to communicate and interact with each other. It acts as a bridge, enabling developers to access certain functionalities or data from an application or platform without having to understand or modify its underlying code.

Think of an API as a waiter in a restaurant. When you go to a restaurant, you don't have to enter the kitchen and cook the meal yourself. Instead, you interact with the waiter, who takes your order, communicates it to the kitchen, and brings your food back to your table. Similarly, an API acts as an intermediary, receiving requests from one software application (the client) and delivering them to another (the server) in a standardized and predictable manner.

APIs come in different forms, but one of the most common types is a web API. Web APIs use the

Hypertext Transfer Protocol (HTTP) to enable communication between applications over the internet. They typically expose a set of endpoints or URLs that represent specific functionalities or resources. By making a request to these endpoints using HTTP methods such as GET, POST, PUT, or DELETE, developers can retrieve data, send data, or perform various operations on the server-side application.

APIs play a crucial role in enabling integration and interoperability between different software systems. They allow developers to leverage existing services, platforms, or functionalities without reinventing the wheel. For example, social media platforms like Facebook and Twitter provide APIs that allow developers to integrate their applications with social features like sharing, authentication, or retrieving user information. This allows developers to enhance their own applications by leveraging the established user base and functionalities of these platforms.

In summary, an API is a set of rules and protocols that enable different software applications to communicate and interact with each other. It acts as an intermediary, allowing developers to access specific functionalities or data from an application or platform without diving into its underlying code. APIs are commonly used in the form of web APIs, which utilize HTTP to facilitate communication over the internet. By leveraging APIs, developers can enhance their own applications, integrate with external services, and build upon the capabilities of existing software systems.

Why are APIs important?

APIs have become a fundamental building block of modern technology ecosystems, and their importance cannot be overstated. Here are several reasons why APIs are crucial in today's digital landscape:

Seamless Integration: APIs enable different software systems to seamlessly communicate and integrate with each other. By providing a standardized interface for interaction, APIs simplify the process of connecting and sharing data between applications, whether they are developed in-house or by third-party providers. This integration capability fosters innovation by allowing developers to combine the strengths of multiple systems and create powerful new solutions.

Rapid Development: APIs accelerate the pace of software development by offering pre-built functionalities and services. Instead of starting from scratch, developers can leverage existing APIs to access features like payment processing, geolocation, or social media integration, saving time and effort. This promotes faster development cycles, reduces development costs, and enables businesses to bring their products and services to market more quickly.

Extensibility and Scalability: APIs provide a scalable foundation for applications. By encapsulating complex functionalities behind a well-designed API, developers can create modular and extensible systems. This modular approach allows businesses to add new features, services, or components without disrupting the existing architecture. It also facilitates collaboration between different teams or organizations, as each can work independently on their designated APIs while ensuring compatibility through agreed-upon interfaces.

Access to Resources and Data: APIs grant developers access to valuable resources and data that are otherwise locked within applications or platforms. Whether it's retrieving weather information, accessing financial data, or querying a database, APIs expose these capabilities in a controlled and secure manner. This accessibility to diverse data sources and services empowers developers to create innovative applications that leverage the wealth of information available across various systems.

Encourages Ecosystems and Partnerships:
APIs foster the development of ecosystems and partnerships within the technology industry. By providing APIs, companies can invite developers and partners to build upon their platforms, expanding their reach and enhancing the value they offer. This collaborative approach promotes innovation, drives developer engagement, and opens up new revenue streams for both platform providers and developers.

In conclusion, APIs are vital in today's digital landscape for enabling seamless integration, accelerating development, promoting extensibility, providing access to resources and data, and fostering ecosystems and partnerships. By embracing APIs, businesses can unlock new opportunities, improve efficiency, and create innovative solutions that leverage the power of interconnected systems.

Common use cases for APIs

APIs find application across a wide range of industries and use cases, enabling developers to leverage the capabilities of existing systems and services. Here are some common use cases where APIs play a crucial role:

Social Media Integration: Social media platforms such as Facebook, Twitter, and Instagram provide

APIs that allow developers to integrate their applications with social features. These APIs enable functionalities like social login, sharing content, retrieving user data, and posting updates. By integrating with social media APIs, applications can enhance user engagement, leverage social connections, and tap into the vast user bases of these platforms.

Payment Gateways: APIs offered by payment gateways like PayPal, Stripe, and Braintree simplify the process of accepting online payments. These APIs enable developers to integrate secure payment processing into their applications, handling tasks such as processing credit card transactions, managing subscriptions, and handling refunds. By utilizing payment gateways' APIs, businesses can provide a seamless and secure payment experience to their customers.

Maps and Geolocation Services: APIs provided by mapping and geolocation services like Google Maps, Mapbox, and OpenStreetMap offer developers access to powerful mapping and geolocation functionalities. Through these APIs, developers can embed maps, retrieve location data, calculate distances, and obtain directions in their applications. These APIs find use in various industries, including transportation, logistics, ride-sharing, and delivery services.

Weather Data: Weather APIs, such as those provided by OpenWeatherMap and AccuWeather, allow developers to access real-time and forecast weather information. By integrating weather APIs into their applications, developers can provide users with weather updates, build personalized weather alerts, and incorporate weather data into planning and decision-making processes across industries like travel, agriculture, and outdoor activities.

E-commerce and Marketplace Integration: APIs offered by e-commerce platforms like Shopify, WooCommerce, and Amazon Marketplace enable seamless integration with online stores and marketplaces. These APIs empower developers to manage products, process orders, retrieve inventory information, and synchronize data between their applications and e-commerce platforms. This integration streamlines the selling process and enables businesses to reach a broader customer base.

Cloud Services and Infrastructure: Cloud service providers like Amazon Web Services (AWS), Microsoft Azure, and Google Cloud Platform offer APIs to manage cloud resources, including virtual machines, storage, databases, and serverless functions. These APIs enable developers to programmatically provision, monitor, and control cloud resources, automating infrastructure management and facilitating the development and deployment of scalable applications.

These are just a few examples of the numerous use cases where APIs play a vital role. From social media integration to payment gateways, mapping services to weather data, and e-commerce to cloud services, APIs provide developers with the means to enhance their applications, access valuable functionalities, and integrate with a wide array of systems and services, fostering innovation and driving efficiency across industries.

Chapter 2: Fundamentals of Web Technologies

Basics of HTTP

HTTP (Hypertext Transfer Protocol) is the foundation of communication on the World Wide Web. It is a protocol that enables the transfer of data between clients (such as web browsers) and servers. Understanding the basics of HTTP is essential for working with APIs. Here are the key concepts to grasp:

Client-Server Communication: HTTP follows a client-server model, where the client (usually a web browser or application) sends requests to a server and receives responses in return. The client initiates a request, and the server processes it and sends back a response.

Request-Response Cycle: The HTTP request-response cycle consists of two main parts: the request sent by the client and the corresponding response from the server. The client initiates a request by specifying the HTTP method (e.g., GET, POST, PUT, DELETE) and the URL of the resource it wants to interact with. The server processes the request, performs the necessary operations, and returns an HTTP response with a status code and optional data.

URL Structure: URLs (Uniform Resource Locators) are used to identify resources on the web. A URL consists of several components, including the protocol (http:// or https://), the domain or IP address of the server, the path to the resource, and optional query parameters. For example, in the URL "http://example.com/api/users?name=john", "http://" represents the protocol, "example.com" is the domain, "/api/users" is the path, and "?name=john" is a query parameter.

HTTP Methods: HTTP provides a set of methods to define the type of operation the client wants to perform on a resource. The most commonly used methods include:

GET: Retrieves a resource from the server.
POST: Sends data to the server to create a new resource.
PUT: Updates an existing resource on the server.
DELETE: Deletes a resource from the server.

Headers: HTTP headers provide additional information about the request or response. Headers can include metadata, authentication tokens, content types, and more. Common headers include "Content-Type" (specifying the format of the data),

"Authorization" (providing authentication credentials), and "Accept" (indicating the desired response format).

Status Codes: HTTP responses include status codes that indicate the outcome of the request. Status codes are three-digit numbers grouped into categories. Some common status codes include:

200: OK (Successful request)
201: Created (Successful resource creation)
400: Bad Request (Invalid request)
401: Unauthorized (Authentication required)
404: Not Found (Requested resource not found)
500: Internal Server Error (Server encountered an error)

Understanding the basics of HTTP provides a foundation for working with APIs. By grasping concepts like client-server communication, the request-response cycle, URL structure, HTTP methods, headers, and status codes, you'll be equipped to interact effectively with APIs and understand the responses they provide.

Understanding URLs

URLs (Uniform Resource Locators) are an essential component of the web and serve as addresses that identify resources such as web pages, images, documents, or API endpoints. Understanding the structure and components of URLs is crucial when working with APIs. Here are the key aspects to grasp:

Protocol: The protocol specifies the set of rules and conventions used for communication. The most common protocol for the web is HTTP (Hypertext Transfer Protocol). Another commonly used protocol is HTTPS (HTTP Secure), which adds a layer of encryption for secure communication. The protocol is denoted at the beginning of a URL, such as "http://" or "https://".

Domain: The domain identifies the specific website or server hosting the resource. It is also referred to as the hostname. For example, in the URL "https://www.example.com/api/users", "www.example.com" is the domain. The domain can also be represented by an IP address, such as "https://192.168.0.1/api/users".

Path: The path specifies the location of the resource within the server's file system or API endpoints. It comes after the domain and is separated by slashes ("/"). For instance, in the URL "https://www.example.com/api/users", "/api/users" is the path. The path can include multiple levels of directories or segments to navigate to specific resources.

Query Parameters: Query parameters are additional information appended to the end of a URL to provide specific instructions or data to the server. They are preceded by a question mark ("?") and separated by ampersands ("&"). For example, in the URL "https://www.example.com/api/users? name=john&age=25", the query parameters are "name=john" and "age=25". Query parameters allow customization and filtering of requests, enabling specific data retrieval or operations.

Fragment Identifier: A fragment identifier, denoted by a hash symbol ("#"), refers to a specific section within a resource. It is commonly used in web pages to navigate to specific sections or elements within a long document or webpage. For instance, in the URL "https://www.example.com/page#section3", the fragment identifier is "section3".

URL Encoding: URLs may contain special characters or reserved characters (such as spaces, slashes, or ampersands) that have special meanings. To include these characters in a URL, they need to be encoded using percent-encoding. For example, spaces are represented as "%20", and ampersands are represented as "%26". URL encoding ensures that URLs are correctly interpreted by servers and browsers.

Understanding the components of URLs is essential when working with APIs as they dictate how requests are made and resources are identified. By comprehending the protocol, domain, path, query parameters, fragment identifier, and URL encoding, you can construct and interpret URLs effectively, interact with APIs, and retrieve the desired resources or perform specific operations on them.

Introduction to JSON

JSON (JavaScript Object Notation) is a lightweight and widely used data interchange format. It provides a simple and human-readable way to represent data structures as text. JSON has become the de facto standard for data exchange in web APIs due to its simplicity and compatibility with various programming languages. Here are the key aspects to understand about JSON:

Data Structure: JSON represents data in a hierarchical structure composed of key-value pairs. The data can be organized into objects, arrays, and primitive values. An object is enclosed in curly braces ({}) and consists of key-value pairs, where the key is a string and the value can be any JSON data type. Arrays, denoted by square brackets ([]), hold an ordered list of values. Primitive values in JSON include strings, numbers, booleans, null, and sometimes special values like dates.

Syntax: JSON follows a straightforward syntax. Keys and string values are enclosed in double quotation marks (""). Values can be strings, numbers, booleans (true or false), null, objects, or arrays. Objects and arrays can nest other objects, arrays, or primitive values. Commas (,) separate key-value pairs or elements within arrays, and colons (:) separate keys from their corresponding values. JSON does not support comments.

Example JSON Object:

```
{
  "name": "John Doe",
  "age": 30,
  "isStudent": false,
  "courses": ["Math", "English", "Science"],
  "address": {
    "street": "123 Main St",
    "city": "Exampleville"
  }
}
```

Parsing and Serialization: In programming, JSON can be parsed (converted) from a string into a native data structure or serialized (converted) from a data structure into a JSON string. Most programming languages provide built-in functions or libraries to parse and serialize JSON. Parsing JSON allows accessing and manipulating the data within an application, while serialization is used for sending JSON data to an API or storing it in a file.

Usage in APIs: JSON is widely used in web APIs for data exchange. APIs often send responses in JSON format, allowing clients to retrieve data in a structured manner. Similarly, clients can send JSON payloads in API requests to provide data or update resources. JSON's simplicity, human-readability, and compatibility with various programming languages make it an ideal choice for data transmission in API communication.

JSON Schema: JSON Schema is a tool for validating the structure and integrity of JSON data. It provides a way to define the expected structure, data types, and constraints of JSON objects. JSON Schema enables developers to enforce rules and validate incoming or outgoing JSON data against a predefined schema, ensuring data consistency and integrity in API interactions.

JSON's simplicity, human-readability, and interoperability have made it a widely adopted format for data exchange in web APIs. By understanding the data structure, syntax, parsing, serialization, and its usage in APIs, you'll be well-equipped to work with JSON data in API integrations and utilize the power of JSON for efficient data exchange and manipulation.

Chapter 3: Exploring RESTful APIs

Overview of REST architecture

REST (Representational State Transfer) is an architectural style for designing networked applications. It provides a set of principles and constraints that facilitate the development of scalable, stateless, and interoperable web services. Understanding the basics of REST architecture is essential for working with RESTful APIs. Here are the key concepts to grasp:

Resource-Oriented Design: REST is based on a resource-oriented design approach, where resources represent entities or objects in the system. Resources are identified by unique URIs (Uniform Resource Identifiers) and can be accessed and manipulated using standard HTTP methods. For example, in an e-commerce system, products, customers, and orders can be considered as resources.

Stateless Communication: REST is stateless, meaning that each request from a client to a server contains all the necessary information to process that request. The server does not maintain any client-specific context between requests. This design principle enhances scalability, as servers can handle requests independently without relying on previous interactions.

Uniform Interface: REST relies on a uniform interface, which defines a standard set of HTTP methods to perform operations on resources. The most commonly used methods are GET (retrieve a resource), POST (create a new resource), PUT (update an existing resource), and DELETE (remove a resource). The uniform interface simplifies API design and allows clients and servers to understand each other without prior knowledge.

Representation and Media Types: REST emphasizes the use of different representations to represent resources. A representation is the format in which a resource is transferred over the network, such as JSON, XML, or HTML. Clients and servers negotiate the representation using media types (also known as MIME types) specified in the HTTP "Content-Type" and "Accept" headers.

Stateless Responses: When a client sends a request to a server, the server responds with a representation of the requested resource. The response may include additional metadata, such as headers providing information about caching, content negotiation, or authentication. Like requests, responses in REST are stateless, meaning that each response is self-contained and does not rely on prior requests.

Hypermedia as the Engine of Application State (HATEOAS): HATEOAS is a fundamental principle in REST that allows clients to navigate and discover resources dynamically. It means that API responses include hyperlinks to related resources or actions that clients can follow to interact with the API further. HATEOAS enables the API to evolve over time without breaking client implementations, as clients rely on the provided links rather than hard-coded URLs.

REST architecture provides a scalable and flexible approach to building web services and APIs. By understanding the resource-oriented design, stateless communication, uniform interface, representation and media types, stateless responses, and HATEOAS, you can design and consume RESTful APIs effectively, leveraging the power of HTTP methods and adhering to the principles of the REST architecture.

HTTP methods (GET, POST, PUT, DELETE)

HTTP (Hypertext Transfer Protocol) provides a set of methods that define the type of operation to be performed on a resource. These methods allow clients to interact with servers and perform actions such as retrieving data, creating new resources, updating existing resources, and deleting resources. Here are the commonly used HTTP methods: GET, POST, PUT, and DELETE:

GET: The GET method is used to retrieve a representation of a resource from the server. When a client sends a GET request, the server responds with the requested resource if it exists. GET requests are safe and idempotent, meaning they should not have any side effects on the server and can be repeated without changing the server's state. The GET method is often used to retrieve data from APIs.

POST: The POST method is used to submit data to the server to create a new resource. Clients send POST requests with a payload containing the data to be processed by the server. The server handles the data and typically responds with the newly created resource's representation. POST requests are not idempotent, as submitting the same data multiple times can result in the creation of multiple resources with different identifiers.

PUT: The PUT method is used to update an existing resource on the server. Clients send PUT requests with a payload containing the updated representation of the resource. The server then replaces the existing resource with the new representation or creates it if it doesn't already exist. Like POST, PUT requests are not idempotent. However, if the same request is sent multiple times, it should result in the same final state of the resource.

DELETE: The DELETE method is used to remove a specified resource from the server. Clients send DELETE requests to the URL of the resource they want to delete. The server processes the request and removes the resource if it exists. DELETE requests are not idempotent, as subsequent requests will return an error if the resource has already been deleted.

It's important to note that these HTTP methods should be used according to their intended purpose and adhere to the principles of RESTful API design. Proper usage of these methods ensures a consistent and predictable API behavior, allowing clients to interact with resources in a well-defined manner. Additionally, other HTTP methods such as PATCH (partial updates) and OPTIONS (metadata retrieval) provide additional functionality in specific scenarios but are less commonly used than GET, POST, PUT, and DELETE.

Working with RESTful endpoints

RESTful endpoints are the URLs or routes exposed by a web service or API that allow clients to interact with the server and perform operations on resources. When working with RESTful endpoints, there are several key aspects to consider:

Resource Identification: RESTful endpoints are designed around resources, which represent entities or objects in the system. Each resource is identified by a unique URL or URI (Uniform Resource Identifier). The URL structure typically follows a hierarchical pattern, with different URL segments representing different levels of the resource hierarchy.

HTTP Methods: RESTful endpoints are accessed using HTTP methods, such as GET, POST, PUT, and DELETE. The HTTP method used in a request determines the type of operation to be performed on the resource. For example, GET is used to retrieve a resource, POST to create a new resource, PUT to update an existing resource, and DELETE to remove a resource.

Request Payload: In some cases, HTTP methods like POST and PUT require a payload to be included in the request. The payload contains the data or representation of the resource being created or updated. The payload can be in various formats, such as JSON, XML, or form data, depending on the API's requirements.

Query Parameters: RESTful endpoints often allow the inclusion of query parameters in the URL to customize and filter the results of a request. Query parameters are appended to the URL with a question mark ("?") and separated by ampersands ("&"). They provide additional information to the server, such as sorting, filtering, pagination, or search criteria.

Response Format: The server responds to RESTful endpoint requests with an HTTP response, which includes a status code and optional response data. The response data is typically in a specified format, such as JSON or XML, depending on the API's configuration. Clients can parse and process the response data to retrieve the desired information or perform further actions.

Error Handling: When working with RESTful endpoints, it's important to handle and interpret error responses appropriately. API endpoints may return specific status codes, such as 400 for a bad request or 404 for a resource not found, to indicate errors. Error responses often include additional details or error messages that provide insights into the issue encountered.

Working with RESTful endpoints involves constructing appropriate URLs, selecting the right HTTP methods, including request payloads when necessary, handling query parameters for customization, parsing and processing the response data, and properly handling error responses. By following RESTful principles and leveraging these aspects, you can effectively interact with RESTful APIs and perform operations on resources in a structured and consistent manner.

Chapter 4: Making API Requests

Introduction to cURL and Postman

cURL and Postman are popular tools used by developers and API consumers to interact with APIs and test API endpoints. They provide convenient ways to make HTTP requests, inspect responses, and analyze API behavior. Here's an overview of these tools:

cURL: cURL (Client URL) is a command-line tool available on most operating systems. It allows users to send HTTP requests directly from the terminal or command prompt. cURL supports various protocols, including HTTP, HTTPS, FTP, and more. With cURL, you can specify the HTTP method, headers, request payloads, and other parameters to interact with an API endpoint. It provides a straightforward way to test and debug APIs from the command line.

Postman: Postman is a powerful API development and testing tool that provides a user-friendly interface for making HTTP requests. It offers a rich set of features, including a request builder, request history, environments, authentication management, and response visualization. With Postman, you can easily create and save requests, organize them into collections, and share them with teammates. It supports various authentication methods, such as OAuth and API keys, making it convenient for testing authenticated APIs. Postman also allows you to write and execute test scripts to automate API testing and validation.

Using cURL and Postman provides several benefits when working with APIs:

Quick Testing: Both tools allow for quick and easy testing of API endpoints without the need for complex setup or development.

- Request Customization: You can specify headers, query parameters, request payloads, and other parameters to simulate different scenarios and test various API functionalities.
- Response Inspection: cURL and Postman display detailed response information, including status codes, headers, and response bodies, facilitating debugging and troubleshooting.
- Collaboration: Postman offers features for sharing requests and collections, enabling collaboration among team members during API development and testing.

- Automation: Postman's scripting capabilities allow you to write test scripts and automate API testing, making it useful for continuous integration and deployment workflows.

Whether you prefer a command-line interface or a user-friendly graphical interface, cURL and Postman are valuable tools for working with APIs. They streamline the process of making requests, inspecting responses, and testing API functionality, enhancing productivity and ensuring reliable API interactions.

Sending GET requests

In the context of working with APIs, a GET request is used to retrieve data from a server. It is one of the most commonly used HTTP methods and is considered safe and idempotent, meaning it should not have any side effects on the server and can be repeated without changing the server's state. Here's a more detailed look at sending GET requests:

Anatomy of a GET Request: To send a GET request, you need to specify the URL of the resource you want to retrieve. The URL typically consists of the base API endpoint and additional path segments or query parameters to specify the exact resource or filter the results. For example, in a hypothetical API for retrieving user information, a GET request to retrieve a specific user might have a URL like: https://api.example.com/users/123.

Query Parameters: GET requests often include query parameters in the URL to customize the request or filter the data. Query parameters are appended to the URL using the question mark symbol ("?") and separated by ampersands ("&"). For example, a GET request to retrieve a list of users with a specific role might have a URL like: https://api.example.com/users?role=admin.

Headers: Headers provide additional information about the request, such as the expected response format, authorization credentials, or caching directives. While not required for a basic GET request, headers can be included to convey specific requirements or preferences. Common headers used in GET requests include "Accept" to specify the desired response format (e.g., JSON or XML) and "Authorization" for authentication if required by the API.

Handling the Response: After sending a GET request, the server responds with an HTTP response. The response contains a status code indicating the success or failure of the request (e.g., 200 for a successful request, 404 for a resource not found). Additionally, the response may include response headers providing metadata about the response, such as the content type or cache-control instructions. The response body contains the requested data in the specified format (e.g., JSON or XML). Clients can parse the response body to extract the desired information.

Error Handling: When working with GET requests, it's important to handle and interpret error responses properly. If the requested resource is not found, the server typically responds with a 404 status code. Other possible error scenarios include authentication failures, rate limiting, or server errors. Robust error handling ensures that the client can gracefully handle and present errors to the user when necessary.

Tools for Sending GET Requests: To send GET requests, you can use various tools and libraries. cURL, as mentioned earlier, allows you to send GET requests from the command line using the curl command with the appropriate URL. Postman, with its user-friendly interface, provides a dedicated interface for creating and sending GET requests. Additionally, programming languages often provide HTTP libraries or frameworks that simplify sending GET requests, allowing developers to incorporate API interactions into their applications.

By understanding the anatomy of a GET request, including query parameters, headers, and proper response handling, you can effectively retrieve data from APIs using this HTTP method. Utilizing tools like cURL, Postman, or HTTP libraries in your chosen programming language will further enhance your ability to send GET requests and work with API resources efficiently.

Handling query parameters and headers

When working with APIs, query parameters and headers are essential components for customizing requests and providing additional information to the server. They allow you to tailor the behavior of the API and communicate specific requirements or preferences. Let's explore how to handle query parameters and headers in more detail:

Query Parameters: Query parameters are appended to the URL of a request and are used to pass additional information to the server. They are commonly used for filtering, sorting, pagination, or specifying search criteria. Here are some key points to consider when working with query parameters:

Building the URL: To include query parameters, append a question mark ("?") to the base URL, followed by the parameter key-value pairs separated by ampersands ("&"). For example: https://api.example.com/users? role=admin&status=active.

Encoding: Ensure that query parameter values are properly encoded to handle special characters or spaces. Most programming languages or HTTP libraries provide functions or methods for URL encoding.

Optional Parameters: Query parameters are typically optional and not all parameters need to be included in every request. The server should handle missing parameters gracefully and provide appropriate default behavior.

Headers: Headers provide additional information about the request or convey specific requirements to the server. They can include details such as the expected response format, authorization credentials, caching instructions, or user agent information. Consider the following when working with headers:

Common Headers: Some common headers used in API requests include "Accept" to specify the desired response format (e.g., JSON or XML), "Authorization" for authentication, and "Content-Type" to indicate the format of the request payload, if applicable.

Authorization: If the API requires authentication, you need to include an "Authorization" header with the appropriate credentials. The specific authentication method will determine the structure and content of the header, such as API keys, access tokens, or OAuth tokens.
Custom Headers: APIs may also define custom headers for specific purposes. Refer to the API documentation to understand any additional headers required or recommended for interacting with the API.

Tools and Libraries: Various tools and libraries simplify the handling of query parameters and headers when working with APIs. Postman provides an intuitive interface for adding and modifying query parameters and headers. When using programming languages, HTTP libraries or frameworks often include methods or functions to set query parameters and headers in API requests. Refer to the documentation of the specific library or framework you are using for guidance.

Properly handling query parameters and headers enables you to fine-tune API requests and communicate important details to the server. Whether you are building the URL with query parameters, encoding values, including headers for authentication or customization, or using tools and libraries, mastering the management of these components will enhance your ability to interact effectively with APIs.

Chapter 5: Working with API Responses

Understanding HTTP status codes

HTTP status codes are three-digit numbers returned by the server as part of an HTTP response. They provide information about the status of a request and help the client understand the outcome of the interaction. HTTP status codes are grouped into different categories, each representing a specific type of response. Let's explore the common HTTP status codes and their meanings:

Informational (1xx): Informational status codes indicate that the server has received the request and is continuing to process it. These codes are rarely encountered in API interactions but can be useful for monitoring and debugging purposes.

Success (2xx): Success status codes indicate that the request was successful and the server has processed it as intended. The most common success code is:

- 200 OK: This status code indicates that the request was successful, and the server has returned the requested resource or performed the requested action.

Redirection (3xx):
Redirection status codes indicate that further action needs to be taken to complete the request. Common redirection codes include:

- 301 Moved Permanently: The requested resource has been permanently moved to a new location. The client should update its links or bookmarks.
- 302 Found: The requested resource has been temporarily moved to a different location. The client should continue to use the original URL.
- 304 Not Modified: The requested resource has not changed since the client's last request. The server responds with this code to indicate that the client can use its cached version.

Client Errors (4xx):
Client error status codes indicate that the request was incorrect or could not be fulfilled due to client-side issues. Common client error codes include:

- 400 Bad Request: The server cannot process the request due to malformed syntax or invalid parameters.

- 401 Unauthorized: Authentication is required to access the requested resource. The client needs to provide valid credentials.
- 404 Not Found: The requested resource could not be found on the server.

Server Errors (5xx): Server error status codes indicate that the server encountered an error while processing the request. Common server error codes include:

- 500 Internal Server Error: An unexpected condition occurred on the server, and it was unable to fulfill the request.
- 503 Service Unavailable: The server is temporarily unable to handle the request, typically due to maintenance or high load.

Understanding HTTP status codes allows you to interpret the server's response and take appropriate action based on the outcome of the request. When working with APIs, it's crucial to handle different status codes correctly to handle errors, retry requests, or provide meaningful feedback to users. API documentation often provides details on the expected status codes for specific endpoints and how to handle them.

Parsing JSON responses

JSON (JavaScript Object Notation) is a popular data format used for structuring and exchanging data between a client and a server. When working with APIs, it is common to receive JSON responses from the server. Here's a guide on parsing JSON responses:

JSON Syntax: JSON follows a simple and intuitive syntax. It consists of key-value pairs enclosed in curly braces {}. Keys are strings and must be unique within an object. Values can be strings, numbers, booleans, null, arrays, or nested objects. Arrays are ordered lists of values enclosed in square brackets []. Understanding the basic JSON syntax is essential for parsing responses.

JSON Parsing: Parsing JSON involves extracting data from the JSON response and converting it into a format that can be easily manipulated and used in your application. The process typically involves the following steps:

1. Retrieve the JSON Response: Receive the JSON response from the API after making an HTTP request.
2. Deserialize the JSON: Convert the JSON response into an object or data structure that can be processed in your programming

language. Most programming languages provide built-in libraries or functions for deserializing JSON.

Accessing Data: Access the desired data within the JSON structure using dot notation or square bracket notation. Dot notation is used when accessing properties directly, while square bracket notation is used when the property names are dynamic or contain special characters.

Handle Nested Objects and Arrays: If the JSON response contains nested objects or arrays, navigate through the structure to access the required data.

JSON Parsing Libraries: Most programming languages have libraries or modules that simplify JSON parsing. These libraries provide methods or functions to deserialize JSON and handle data extraction. Some popular JSON parsing libraries include:

- JavaScript: JSON.parse() or libraries like JSON.parse() or JSON.stringify().
- Python: json module or third-party libraries like json or simplejson.
- Java: Jackson, Gson, or org.json libraries.
- Ruby: JSON.parse() or libraries like JSON.parse() or Oj.

Error Handling: When parsing JSON responses, it's important to handle potential errors gracefully.

JSON parsing can fail if the response is not in valid JSON format. Make sure to catch and handle any parsing exceptions to prevent application crashes or unexpected behavior.

Data Validation: It's recommended to validate the parsed JSON data against a predefined schema or structure, especially if the API response format is subject to change. Data validation helps ensure that the response conforms to your expectations and avoids potential issues when processing the data further.

By understanding JSON syntax, using appropriate JSON parsing libraries, and implementing error handling and data validation, you can effectively parse JSON responses from APIs and extract the necessary data for your application.

Error handling and troubleshooting

When working with APIs, error handling and troubleshooting play a crucial role in ensuring smooth interactions and resolving issues effectively. Understanding common error scenarios and implementing robust error handling mechanisms are essential. Here's a guide to error handling and troubleshooting when working with APIs:

HTTP Status Codes: HTTP status codes provide valuable information about the outcome of a request. Familiarize yourself with common HTTP status codes, as discussed in a previous section, to understand the different types of errors and their meanings. Handle status codes appropriately in your application code to provide meaningful feedback to users or take necessary actions.

Error Response Format: APIs often provide error responses in a structured format, typically JSON or XML, containing specific details about the encountered error. The error response may include fields such as error codes, error messages, and additional information to help identify the problem. Refer to the API documentation to understand the expected structure and fields of error responses.

Handling Errors: Implement proper error handling in your code to capture and process API errors. This includes:

Checking for Successful Responses: Verify if the HTTP status code indicates a successful request (2xx range). If not, treat it as an error and proceed with error handling.

Parsing Error Responses: Extract relevant information from the error response, such as error codes or messages, to provide meaningful feedback to users or for troubleshooting purposes.

Graceful Error Messaging: Present user-friendly error messages that convey the issue encountered and provide guidance on possible solutions or next steps.

Retry and Backoff Strategies: For certain types of errors, such as temporary network issues or rate limiting, implement retry mechanisms with appropriate backoff strategies to handle the error condition and avoid overwhelming the API.

Logging and Debugging: Implement logging mechanisms to capture relevant information about API interactions and error conditions. Log error responses, request parameters, and any additional details that can assist in troubleshooting. Effective logging facilitates identifying patterns, pinpointing the root cause of issues, and collaborating with API providers or support teams for resolution.

API Rate Limiting: Some APIs enforce rate limits to prevent abuse and ensure fair usage. If you encounter rate limiting errors, review the API documentation for the specified rate limits and adjust your application's usage accordingly. Implement strategies like request throttling or handling rate limit headers to gracefully handle rate limiting scenarios.

API Documentation and Support: Consult the API documentation for specific error codes, troubleshooting guides, and recommended solutions. APIs often provide extensive documentation that covers common errors, troubleshooting steps, and best practices. If you're unable to resolve an issue through documentation, reach out to the API provider's support channels for further assistance.

By proactively handling errors, parsing error responses, implementing effective logging, and utilizing API documentation and support channels, you can troubleshoot issues efficiently and ensure a robust and reliable integration with the API.

Chapter 6: Authentication and Authorization

Basics of API authentication

API authentication is a crucial aspect of securing API interactions and ensuring that only authorized users or applications can access protected resources. It involves validating the identity of the client making the request and granting access based on credentials or tokens. Let's explore the basics of API authentication:

API Keys: API keys are commonly used for authentication and act as unique identifiers that grant access to the API. They are typically long, randomly generated strings associated with a specific user or application. To use an API key, it is usually included in the request headers or query parameters. API keys are simple to implement and provide a basic level of security for API access.

Token-Based Authentication: Token-based authentication is widely used in APIs and involves exchanging credentials for a token that is then used for subsequent requests. The most common token-based authentication method is OAuth 2.0. The authentication flow typically involves the following steps:

1. Client Authorization: The client (user or application) requests authorization from the API provider.
2. Authorization Grant: The client receives an authorization grant, such as a code or a refresh token, from the API provider.
3. Token Request: The client exchanges the authorization grant for an access token from the API provider.
4. Token Usage: The client includes the access token in the request headers for subsequent API calls.

Basic Authentication: Basic authentication is a simple authentication method where the client includes a username and password in the request headers. Although straightforward, it is less secure compared to other authentication methods because credentials are sent in plain text. It is recommended to use secure communication channels, such as HTTPS, when using basic authentication.

API Authentication Standards: Several authentication standards and protocols exist to enhance API security and interoperability. Some widely used standards include:

- OAuth 2.0: A protocol for authorization that enables secure delegation of user access to APIs.
- OpenID Connect: An authentication layer built on top of OAuth 2.0 that provides user authentication and identity information.
- JSON Web Tokens (JWT): A compact, URL-safe format for representing claims between parties. JWTs can be used for authentication and information exchange.

Two-Factor Authentication (2FA): Two-factor authentication adds an extra layer of security by requiring users to provide additional proof of identity, typically through a secondary device or verification method. Implementing 2FA in API authentication strengthens the security of user accounts and API access.

API Authentication Best Practices: When working with API authentication, consider the following best practices:

- Use Secure Communication: Always communicate with the API over secure channels, such as HTTPS, to encrypt the data exchanged between the client and the server.
- Protect Credentials: Safeguard API keys, access tokens, and other sensitive information. Avoid hardcoding credentials in

the application code or exposing them in public repositories.

- Implement Rate Limiting: Enforce rate limits to prevent abuse and protect your API from malicious or excessive usage.
- Follow API Provider Guidelines: Adhere to the authentication guidelines and recommendations provided by the API provider. Familiarize yourself with the API documentation and any specific requirements or restrictions.

By understanding API authentication methods, implementing secure practices, and adhering to industry standards, you can ensure the integrity and security of your API interactions while granting appropriate access to authorized users or applications.

API keys and tokens

API keys and tokens are commonly used in API authentication to verify the identity of clients and grant access to protected resources. They serve as credentials that allow authorized users or applications to interact with an API. Let's explore the basics of API keys and tokens:

API Keys: API keys are unique identifiers issued by an API provider to clients for authentication and authorization purposes. They are typically long, randomly generated strings associated with a specific user or application. API keys serve as a simple form of authentication, granting access to the API based on the validity of the provided key.

Obtaining API Keys: API keys are typically obtained by registering for an API account or through a developer portal. The API provider generates a unique key for each client.

Including API Keys: API keys are often included in the request headers or query parameters when making API calls. The specific method of including API keys may vary depending on the API provider's guidelines.

Scope and Permissions: API keys may have associated scopes or permissions that determine the level of access granted to the client. Scopes can limit the actions or resources that the client can access, enhancing security.

Access Tokens: Access tokens are temporary credentials issued by an API provider to authorized clients. They are commonly used in token-based authentication mechanisms such as OAuth 2.0. Access tokens offer a more secure and flexible approach compared to API keys.

Obtaining Access Tokens: Access tokens are obtained through an authentication flow that involves exchanging credentials (e.g., username and password) or authorization grants for a token.

Token Usage: Once obtained, the access token is included in the request headers of subsequent API calls. The token serves as proof of the client's authorization to access protected resources.

Token Expiration and Refresh: Access tokens typically have an expiration time. If the token expires, the client can use a refresh token to obtain a new access token without requiring the user to re-enter their credentials.

Differences and Considerations: API keys and access tokens have some differences and considerations to keep in mind:

Security Level: Access tokens offer a higher level of security compared to API keys. Tokens can be limited in scope, have shorter lifetimes, and can be revoked more easily, providing more granular control over API access.

Revocation and Rotation: API keys are generally long-lived and harder to revoke once leaked. In contrast, access tokens can be revoked or invalidated, allowing for better control and security. Tokens can also be rotated periodically to minimize the impact of a compromised token.

User vs. Application Context: API keys are often associated with the entire application, granting access to all users of that application. Access tokens, on the other hand, can be tied to specific user contexts, enabling more fine-grained access control and personalization.

Best Practices: When working with API keys and tokens, consider the following best practices:

- Safeguard Credentials: Treat API keys and access tokens as sensitive information. Store them securely and avoid exposing them in publicly accessible places, such as public repositories or client-side code.
- Use Encryption and Secure Communication: Protect API keys and tokens by transmitting them over secure channels, such as HTTPS, to prevent interception and unauthorized access.
- Token Management: Implement proper token management, including secure storage, token expiration, and revocation mechanisms. Regularly rotate access tokens to minimize potential security risks.
- Regular Auditing: Perform regular audits of API keys and tokens to ensure they are still valid, up-to-date, and only granted to authorized entities. Revoke any unused or compromised credentials.

- Follow Provider Guidelines: Adhere to the API provider's guidelines and recommendations for API key and token usage. Understand their requirements, restrictions, and any specific mechanisms for obtaining or refreshing credentials.

By understanding the distinctions between API keys and access tokens, following best practices for their usage, and prioritizing security, you can effectively authenticate clients and control access to your APIs while ensuring the confidentiality and integrity of your data.

OAuth and user authentication

OAuth (Open Authorization) is an industry-standard protocol used for secure user authentication and authorization in API integrations. It enables users to grant limited access to their protected resources to third-party applications without sharing their credentials directly. Let's explore the basics of OAuth and user authentication:

OAuth Workflow: The OAuth workflow typically involves the following parties:

Resource Owner: The user who owns the protected resources (e.g., social media account, email account).

Client: The third-party application requesting access to the user's resources.
Authorization Server: The server responsible for authenticating the user and issuing access tokens.
Resource Server: The server hosting the protected resources that the client wants to access.
The OAuth workflow consists of the following steps:

1. Client Registration: The client registers with the authorization server, obtaining client credentials (client ID and client secret).
2. User Authorization: The client redirects the user to the authorization server, where the user authenticates and grants consent to the client.
3. Authorization Grant: The authorization server issues an authorization grant to the client.
4. Access Token Request: The client exchanges the authorization grant with the authorization server for an access token.
5. Accessing Protected Resources: The client includes the access token in API requests to the resource server, which verifies the token and provides access to the requested resources.

User Authentication: OAuth involves user authentication to verify the user's identity and obtain their consent. User authentication can take various forms, such as:

- Username and Password: The user provides their username and password directly to the authorization server for authentication.
- Single Sign-On (SSO): If the user is already authenticated through a centralized identity provider, OAuth can leverage the existing authentication session.
- Social Media Authentication: OAuth can utilize social media platforms (e.g., Facebook, Google) as identity providers, allowing users to authenticate using their existing social media accounts.

Scopes and Permissions: OAuth allows users to grant specific permissions to the client application through the use of scopes. Scopes define the extent of access that the client has to the user's resources. For example, a social media OAuth flow may include scopes like read posts, publish content, or access friend list. Scopes enable fine-grained control over resource access.

Refresh Tokens: To minimize the lifespan of access tokens and enhance security, OAuth supports the use of refresh tokens. Refresh tokens are long-lived credentials that enable the client to obtain new access tokens without requiring user interaction. When an access token expires, the client can use a refresh token to obtain a new access token from the authorization server.

User Consent and Security: OAuth prioritizes user consent and security. Users have the ability to review and revoke the permissions granted to the client at any time. OAuth also ensures secure communication by utilizing encryption protocols (e.g., HTTPS) and requiring the use of secure channels for token exchange.

Best Practices: When implementing OAuth and user authentication, consider the following best practices:

- Use Well-Established Libraries and Frameworks: Utilize trusted OAuth libraries or frameworks provided by your programming language or platform. These libraries handle the complexities of the OAuth protocol and help ensure secure implementation.
- Protect Client Secrets: Safeguard client secrets (client ID and client secret) by storing them securely and avoiding exposure in publicly accessible locations.
- Keep Tokens Confidential: Access tokens and refresh tokens should be treated as sensitive information. Store them securely and transmit them over secure channels.
- Implement Token Expiration and Revocation: Enforce token expiration and provide mechanisms to revoke access tokens and refresh tokens when needed.

Regularly rotate client secrets and refresh
tokens to enhance security.

- Follow OAuth 2.0 Specifications: Adhere to
  the specifications defined in the OAuth 2.0
  protocol and the guidelines provided by the
  API providers. Understand the specific
  OAuth flow and requirements for the APIs
  you are integrating with.

By understanding OAuth workflows, following best
practices, and prioritizing user consent and
security, you can implement secure user
authentication and authorization in your API
integrations while providing a seamless experience
for your users.

Chapter 7: API Design Best Practices

Planning your API

Planning is a crucial phase in developing an API as it lays the foundation for a successful and well-designed API. It involves carefully considering various aspects of your API to ensure it meets the needs of your users and provides a great developer experience. Let's explore the key considerations when planning your API:

Identify Use Cases and Goals: Start by identifying the primary use cases and goals of your API. Determine the problem you aim to solve and the value your API will provide to its users. Understanding the use cases will help you define the scope and functionalities of your API.

Define API Resources: Identify the resources that your API will expose. Resources represent the data entities or services that users can interact with through your API. For example, in an e-commerce API, resources might include products, orders, and customers.

Design Data Model and Schema: Create a well-defined data model that represents the structure and relationships of your API resources. Consider the attributes, relationships, and data types of each resource. Document the data model using a schema language such as JSON Schema or GraphQL Schema.

Choose API Paradigm and Architecture: Select the appropriate API paradigm and architecture that aligns with your use cases and goals. Common paradigms include REST (Representational State Transfer) and GraphQL. Consider factors such as the flexibility of data retrieval, performance requirements, and scalability.

Define API Endpoints and Operations: Based on the identified resources, define the API endpoints that will allow users to interact with your API. Determine the supported operations for each endpoint, such as GET, POST, PUT, and DELETE, to enable data retrieval, creation, modification, and deletion.

Decide on Request and Response Formats: Specify the request and response formats that your API will support. Common formats include JSON (JavaScript Object Notation) and XML (eXtensible Markup Language). Consider the simplicity, readability, and ease of parsing for developers using your API.

Versioning and Backward Compatibility: Plan for versioning and backward compatibility to ensure a smooth evolution of your API over time. Define a versioning strategy, such as using a version number in the API URL or request headers. Consider how changes to the API will affect existing clients and provide mechanisms to handle backward compatibility.

Documentation and Developer Experience: Develop comprehensive and user-friendly documentation for your API. Clearly explain the purpose, capabilities, and usage of each endpoint. Include code examples, tutorials, and interactive tools to facilitate developer onboarding and integration. Consider providing a sandbox environment for testing and experimentation.

Authentication and Authorization: Determine the authentication and authorization mechanisms your API will employ to protect resources and ensure secure access. Evaluate options such as API keys, OAuth, or JWT (JSON Web Tokens) based authentication based on your security requirements.

Rate Limiting and Usage Policies: Consider implementing rate limiting and usage policies to manage API traffic and prevent abuse. Define the rate limits for different API endpoints and communicate them clearly to developers. Monitor and enforce these limits to maintain the performance and availability of your API.

Error Handling and Reporting: Define a consistent and informative approach to handle errors that occur during API interactions. Design clear error messages and status codes to help developers troubleshoot issues effectively. Consider providing error reporting mechanisms, such as logging or analytics, to gather insights on API usage and errors.

Testing and Quality Assurance: Create a testing strategy to ensure the reliability and functionality of your API. Implement unit tests, integration tests, and end-to-end tests to validate API behavior. Consider using tools like Postman, Swagger, or automated testing frameworks to streamline your testing process.

By carefully planning your API, considering these key aspects, and documenting your decisions, you can create a well-structured, user-friendly, and robust API that meets the needs of your developers and empowers them to build innovative applications on top of your platform.

Choosing appropriate endpoints and methods

When designing your API, selecting appropriate endpoints and methods is crucial for providing a well-organized and intuitive interface to your users. By carefully considering the functionality and purpose of your API, you can choose the right endpoints and methods that align with the requirements of your application. Here are some key considerations to help you make informed decisions:

Resource-Centric Design: Adopt a resource-centric design approach where API endpoints represent the resources that users interact with. Identify the core entities or data objects in your system and map them to meaningful and intuitive endpoint URLs. For example, if you have a blog API, endpoints like /posts, /users, and /comments can represent the corresponding resources.

RESTful Principles: Consider following REST (Representational State Transfer) principles when designing your endpoints. REST encourages the use of standardized HTTP methods to perform specific operations on resources. The most commonly used HTTP methods are:

- GET: Retrieve a resource or a collection of resources.
- POST: Create a new resource.
- PUT: Update or replace an existing resource.
- DELETE: Delete a resource.

CRUD Operations: Map your API endpoints to CRUD (Create, Read, Update, Delete) operations for the underlying resources. This mapping helps ensure a consistent and intuitive API design. For example:

- /products (GET): Retrieve a list of products.
- /products/{id} (GET): Retrieve a specific product.
- /products (POST): Create a new product.
- /products/{id} (PUT): Update an existing product.
- /products/{id} (DELETE): Delete a product.

Singular vs. Plural Endpoint Names: Consider whether your endpoints should use singular or plural names. Singular names are appropriate when working with individual resources, while plural names are suitable for collections or groups of resources. For example, /user can represent a single user, while /users can represent a collection of users.

Nested Resources: Decide if your API should support nested resources. Nested resources are useful when there is a hierarchical relationship between entities. For example, /users/{id}/posts can retrieve all posts associated with a specific user.

Custom Actions: Determine if your API requires custom actions beyond the standard CRUD operations. Custom actions represent additional functionality that doesn't fit neatly into the basic resource operations. Use descriptive and meaningful names for custom actions. For example, /products/{id}/publish can trigger a custom action to publish a product.

Versioning: Plan for versioning your API to allow for future changes and updates without breaking existing client integrations. Consider incorporating the version number into the URL structure or request headers. For example, /v1/products can represent version 1 of the products endpoint.

Consistency and Simplicity: Strive for consistency and simplicity in your endpoint design. Use clear and descriptive names that accurately represent the purpose of each endpoint. Avoid overly complex or convoluted URL structures that may confuse users.

Documentation and Developer Experience: Thoroughly document your chosen endpoints and methods in your API documentation. Provide clear explanations, example requests and responses, and any specific requirements or limitations for each endpoint. Offer interactive documentation tools like Swagger or Postman to enhance the developer experience.

Consider Scalability and Performance: Keep scalability and performance in mind when designing endpoints. Avoid creating overly granular endpoints that could result in a large number of API calls for simple operations. Consider pagination, filtering, and sorting options for retrieving collections of resources efficiently.

By carefully selecting appropriate endpoints and methods, following RESTful principles, and considering the specific requirements of your API, you can create a well-structured and intuitive interface for your users, enhancing the usability and effectiveness of your API.

Versioning and documentation

Versioning and documentation play a crucial role in maintaining the stability, compatibility, and usability of your API. They ensure that developers can effectively understand and integrate with your API, even as it evolves over time. Let's explore the key considerations when it comes to versioning and documentation:

Versioning Strategies: Choose a versioning strategy that best suits your API's needs. Common strategies include:

- URL Versioning: Incorporate the version number in the URL structure (e.g., /v1/endpoint) to differentiate between different versions of your API.
- Request Header Versioning: Include the version number in the request headers (e.g., Accept-Version: v1) to indicate the desired API version.
- Media Type Versioning: Use different media types (e.g., application/vnd.yourapi.v1+json) to represent different versions of your API.

Backward Compatibility: Ensure backward compatibility to avoid breaking existing client integrations when introducing new versions. Consider the following practices:

Avoid Removing or Changing Existing Functionality: Once an endpoint or method is released, strive to maintain its behavior unless absolutely necessary.

Deprecation: Clearly communicate when certain features or endpoints will be deprecated and provide developers with a timeline for migration to newer versions.

Versioning Support: Include mechanisms to allow clients to specify the desired API version and gracefully handle requests for deprecated versions.

Comprehensive Documentation: Develop comprehensive and well-structured documentation to assist developers in understanding and integrating with your API. Key aspects of effective documentation include:

- Getting Started Guide: Provide a concise guide that outlines the basic steps required to get started with your API, including authentication and making the first API call.
- API Reference: Document each endpoint, including its purpose, supported methods, parameters, request and response formats, and example usage.
- Code Examples: Include code snippets or sample requests and responses to illustrate how to interact with your API using different programming languages or frameworks.
- Authentication and Authorization: Explain the authentication and authorization mechanisms required to access protected resources.
- Error Handling: Describe the possible errors that can occur during API interactions and provide guidance on how to handle and interpret these errors.

Interactive Tools and Sandbox: Enhance the developer experience by providing interactive tools, such as a sandbox environment or an API console. These tools allow developers to explore and test your API endpoints without making actual production requests. It facilitates experimentation and helps developers understand the behavior of your API.

Developer Support: Offer developer support channels, such as a dedicated email address or community forums, to address developer questions, provide clarifications, and gather feedback. Promptly respond to developer inquiries and consider establishing a knowledge base or FAQ section to address common queries.

Update Documentation with API Changes: As your API evolves, keep your documentation up to date. Ensure that any changes to endpoints, methods, parameters, or responses are reflected in the documentation promptly. Communicate the changes clearly and provide migration guides or version-specific documentation for developers using different API versions.

Organization and Readability: Ensure that your documentation is well-organized, easily navigable, and visually appealing. Use clear headings, sections, and sub-sections to structure the content. Provide a search functionality within your documentation to help developers quickly find the information they need.

Documentation Maintenance: Consider documentation as an ongoing effort. Regularly review and update your documentation to incorporate user feedback, address common issues, and add new features or enhancements. Make documentation maintenance a part of your development and release processes.

By implementing a robust versioning strategy, creating comprehensive documentation, and maintaining backward compatibility, you can provide developers with the necessary resources to integrate smoothly with your API, leading to improved adoption and satisfaction.

Chapter 8: Testing and Debugging APIs

Unit testing APIs

Unit testing is a critical aspect of developing reliable and robust APIs. It allows you to verify the individual components and functionality of your API in isolation, ensuring that they work as intended. Here are some key considerations for unit testing your APIs:

Identify Testable Units: Break down your API into smaller, testable units. This could include individual endpoints, request/response handling logic, data validation, authentication mechanisms, and error handling. Each unit should be isolated and independent, allowing for focused testing.

Choose a Testing Framework: Select a suitable testing framework that supports API testing. Popular frameworks such as pytest, JUnit, and NUnit offer features specifically designed for API testing. These frameworks provide utilities to make HTTP requests, assert response values, and handle test assertions.

Write Test Cases: Create test cases that cover various scenarios and use cases of your API. Test cases should include positive and negative scenarios, boundary cases, and edge cases to ensure thorough testing. Consider testing different HTTP methods, handling of query parameters, headers, and authentication mechanisms.

Mock External Dependencies: To isolate your API unit tests, mock external dependencies such as databases, third-party services, or other APIs. Mocking these dependencies allows you to focus solely on testing the specific functionality of your API without relying on external resources.

Test Data Setup and Teardown: Ensure proper setup and teardown of test data. Set up the necessary data and state required for each test case to execute independently. After the test completes, clean up any created data or revert any changes made during the test to maintain a clean and predictable test environment.

Test Assertions: Perform assertions on the API responses to validate the expected behavior. Assert the HTTP status codes, response payloads, headers, and any other relevant data. Compare the actual values with the expected values defined in your test cases to determine if the API is functioning correctly.

Error Handling and Exception Testing: Test error handling and exception scenarios to ensure your API responds appropriately to unexpected situations. Validate that error responses contain the correct status codes, error messages, and any additional information required for debugging and troubleshooting.

Automation and Continuous Integration: Automate your unit tests and integrate them into your continuous integration (CI) process. This allows you to run tests automatically whenever changes are made to your codebase. Use CI tools such as Jenkins, Travis CI, or CircleCI to set up automated builds and test execution.

Test Coverage: Strive for adequate test coverage to ensure that your tests exercise the majority of your API's codebase. Aim to cover critical paths, edge cases, and error scenarios. Use code coverage analysis tools to measure the percentage of code covered by your tests and identify areas that require additional testing.

Test Reporting and Monitoring: Generate test reports to track the results of your unit tests. Monitor test execution metrics, including the number of passing and failing tests, execution time, and test coverage. Use these reports and metrics to identify areas of improvement and track the overall health of your API.

Continuous Test Maintenance: Maintain your unit tests as your API evolves. Update tests to accommodate changes in functionality, additions of new endpoints, or modifications to existing behavior. Regularly review and refactor your test suite to ensure its effectiveness and efficiency.

By incorporating unit testing into your API development process, you can identify and fix issues early, ensure the reliability of your API, and provide a solid foundation for further testing and integration.

Debugging API issues

Debugging is an essential skill when it comes to resolving issues and ensuring the proper functioning of your API. When encountering problems, having effective debugging techniques can help you identify and address the root causes efficiently. Here are some key considerations for debugging API issues:

Understand the Problem: Start by gathering information about the issue at hand. Identify the specific symptoms, error messages, unexpected behavior, or performance degradation. Reproduce the problem consistently to understand its scope and impact.

Check API Documentation and Specifications:
Refer to your API documentation and specifications
to ensure that you fully understand the expected
behavior of the API. Verify that you are correctly
using the endpoints, parameters, headers, and
authentication mechanisms as specified.

Review Logs and Error Messages: Inspect the
logs and error messages generated by your API.
Logs can provide valuable insights into what
happened during API requests and responses. Pay
attention to any error codes, stack traces, or
exception messages that can pinpoint the source of
the issue.

Enable Debugging Output: Enable debugging
output or verbose mode in your API framework or
server configuration. This can provide additional
information about the internal processing of your
API, such as request/response payloads, headers,
and any intermediate steps.

Use Debugging Tools: Utilize specialized
debugging tools and utilities to aid in
troubleshooting API issues. Tools like Postman,
cURL, or browser developer consoles can help you
inspect and analyze API requests and responses.
Use these tools to validate the data being sent and
received, including headers, payloads, and
response times.

Test Incrementally: Break down the problematic API call into smaller, incremental tests. Test each component independently, ensuring that each part functions as expected. By narrowing down the problem scope, you can isolate the source of the issue more effectively.

Examine Network Traffic: Inspect the network traffic between the client and server. Use network monitoring tools like Wireshark or browser network tabs to capture and analyze the API requests and responses. Pay attention to the headers, data payloads, and any anomalies that may indicate the cause of the issue.

Validate Inputs and Outputs: Double-check the inputs and outputs of your API. Ensure that the request payloads, query parameters, and headers are correctly formed and comply with the expected format. Similarly, validate that the API responses conform to the specified structure and data types.

Test with Different Environments and Configurations: Test your API in various environments and configurations to identify if the issue is specific to certain setups. This can include testing in different operating systems, browsers, network environments, or third-party integrations.

Collaborate and Seek Assistance: If you're unable to resolve the issue on your own, reach out to your team members, community forums, or developer support channels. Explain the problem clearly, provide relevant details, and share any findings from your debugging process. Collaborating with others can bring fresh perspectives and insights to help solve the problem.

Fix, Test, and Validate: Once you've identified the root cause of the issue, implement the necessary fixes in your API codebase. Test the modified code thoroughly, ensuring that the issue is resolved and that the changes haven't introduced any new problems. Validate the fix with the original use case that led to the issue to ensure it's fully resolved.

Document the Debugging Process: Keep a record of the debugging process, including the steps you took, the issues encountered, and the solutions implemented. Documenting the debugging process can serve as a valuable resource for future reference and help in troubleshooting similar issues.

By employing systematic debugging techniques, utilizing appropriate tools, and collaborating with others, you can effectively identify and resolve API issues, ensuring the smooth operation and reliability of your API.

Using API testing tools

API testing tools provide developers with powerful capabilities to automate the testing and validation of APIs. These tools offer a range of features that streamline the testing process, improve efficiency, and ensure the quality of your API implementation. Here are some key considerations when using API testing tools:

Selecting the Right Tool: Choose an API testing tool that aligns with your project requirements, programming language, and testing objectives. Some popular API testing tools include Postman, SoapUI, Insomnia, JMeter, and Newman. Evaluate the features, ease of use, integration capabilities, and community support of each tool before making a selection.

Creating Test Suites: Organize your API tests into logical test suites. Test suites help you group related tests and execute them together, enabling efficient test management and execution. Structure your test suites based on functional areas, use cases, or specific endpoints to facilitate better organization and maintainability.

Defining Test Cases: Create test cases that cover various scenarios and use cases of your API. Test cases should encompass positive and negative scenarios, boundary cases, and error conditions. Define the expected inputs, execute API requests with the defined inputs, and verify the responses against the expected outputs.

Configuring Test Environments: Configure test environments to replicate real-world conditions for your API. This includes setting up test databases, third-party integrations, authentication mechanisms, and any other dependencies required for accurate testing. Test environments should closely resemble the production environment to ensure realistic results.

Automating Tests: Leverage the automation capabilities of API testing tools to execute tests automatically. Automation eliminates manual effort, allows for repeated testing, and accelerates the testing process. Write test scripts using the tool's scripting language or use a visual interface to define test flows and assertions.

Parameterization and Data-Driven Testing: Utilize parameterization and data-driven testing features to execute tests with different inputs and datasets. Parameterization allows you to replace specific values with variables, enabling test execution with various data combinations. Data-driven testing enables you to use external data sources, such as spreadsheets or databases, as inputs for your API tests.

Assertions and Validation: Leverage the built-in assertion capabilities of API testing tools to validate the responses. Assertions allow you to compare actual API responses against expected values or predefined rules. Verify HTTP status codes, response payloads, headers, and other relevant data to ensure the API behaves as intended.

Test Reporting and Analysis: Generate test reports to track the results and analyze the outcome of your API tests. Test reports provide valuable insights into test execution status, test coverage, and any failures or errors encountered. Analyze the reports to identify patterns, trends, and areas that require further attention.

Integration with Continuous Integration (CI) Systems: Integrate your API testing tool with your CI system, such as Jenkins, Travis CI, or CircleCI, to incorporate API tests into your automated build and deployment process. This allows you to automatically trigger tests whenever changes are made to your API codebase and obtain immediate feedback on the build status.

Collaboration and Sharing: Leverage collaboration features offered by API testing tools to share test suites, test cases, and test results with your team. Collaborative features enable team members to work together, review tests, provide feedback, and share testing artifacts, improving overall productivity and quality.

Regular Maintenance and Updates: Regularly update and maintain your test suites as your API evolves. Modify existing tests to accommodate changes in functionality, endpoints, or expected behavior. Add new tests to cover new features or enhancements. Regularly review and refactor your test suite to ensure optimal performance and maintainability.

By leveraging the features and capabilities of API testing tools, you can automate your testing process, ensure comprehensive test coverage, and achieve a higher level of confidence in the quality and reliability of your API implementation.

Chapter 9: API Security

Common security threats

APIs are vulnerable to various security threats that can compromise the confidentiality, integrity, and availability of data and services. Understanding these threats is crucial for developing secure and robust APIs. Here are some common security threats you should be aware of:

Injection Attacks: Injection attacks occur when untrusted data is sent to an API without proper validation or sanitization. This can lead to malicious code execution, data breaches, or unauthorized access. Examples include SQL injection, XML/XXE injection, and OS command injection. Prevent injection attacks by using parameterized queries, input validation, and output encoding.

Authentication and Authorization Vulnerabilities: Weak authentication and authorization mechanisms can allow unauthorized access to API resources. Common vulnerabilities include weak passwords, predictable session tokens, inadequate access controls, and improper handling of user identities. Implement strong authentication protocols, enforce password complexity, use secure session management techniques, and apply fine-grained access controls.

Cross-Site Scripting (XSS): XSS attacks occur when malicious scripts are injected into webpages served by the API, and subsequently executed by unsuspecting users' browsers. This can lead to the theft of sensitive information or the hijacking of user sessions. Prevent XSS attacks by validating and sanitizing user-generated content, implementing content security policies, and utilizing output encoding.

Cross-Site Request Forgery (CSRF): CSRF attacks trick authenticated users into unknowingly performing actions on an API without their consent. This can result in unauthorized transactions, data modification, or account takeover. Mitigate CSRF attacks by implementing anti-CSRF tokens, validating referrer headers, and using unique, unpredictable request identifiers.

Denial of Service (DoS) Attacks: DoS attacks aim to disrupt the availability of an API by overwhelming it with a high volume of requests or resource-intensive operations. This can result in degraded performance, unresponsiveness, or complete downtime. Protect against DoS attacks by implementing rate limiting, request throttling, and monitoring traffic for anomalies.

Man-in-the-Middle (MitM) Attacks: MitM attacks intercept and modify communication between an API and its clients, allowing attackers to eavesdrop, manipulate data, or impersonate legitimate users. Implement secure communication channels using protocols such as HTTPS/TLS to prevent data interception and employ proper certificate validation.

Insecure Direct Object References (IDOR): IDOR vulnerabilities occur when an API exposes internal object references without proper authorization checks. Attackers can manipulate these references to access unauthorized resources or sensitive information. Implement access controls based on user roles and permissions, and use indirect object references that are not directly tied to internal identifiers.

Insecure Deserialization: Insecure deserialization vulnerabilities arise when APIs accept and process serialized data from untrusted sources. Attackers can exploit this weakness to execute arbitrary code, perform remote code execution, or cause denial of service. Validate and sanitize serialized data, implement proper input validation, and use libraries or frameworks with built-in deserialization protections.

Information Disclosure: Information disclosure vulnerabilities expose sensitive information such as API keys, credentials, or internal system details to unauthorized parties. Regularly review your API responses, error messages, and logging mechanisms to ensure they don't inadvertently disclose sensitive information.

Insufficient Logging and Monitoring: Lack of proper logging and monitoring can hinder the detection and response to security incidents. Implement robust logging mechanisms to capture important events and anomalies. Employ monitoring solutions that detect suspicious activities, analyze logs, and provide real-time alerts.

Data Privacy and GDPR Compliance: Ensure compliance with data privacy regulations such as the General Data Protection Regulation (GDPR). Properly handle and protect sensitive user data, obtain explicit user consent for data processing, and provide mechanisms for users to access, modify, or delete their personal information.

To mitigate these security threats, it is essential to adopt secure coding practices, conduct regular security assessments, implement strong authentication and authorization mechanisms, use encryption for data in transit and at rest, and keep abreast of security best practices and emerging threats. Regularly update your API infrastructure and dependencies to address security vulnerabilities promptly.

Securing API endpoints

Securing API endpoints is crucial to protect sensitive data, prevent unauthorized access, and maintain the integrity of your API. By implementing robust security measures, you can ensure that only authenticated and authorized users can access and interact with your API. Here are some key considerations for securing API endpoints:

Authentication: Implement a strong authentication mechanism to verify the identity of API consumers. This can include using techniques such as API keys, tokens, or username/password authentication. Consider more advanced methods like OAuth or OpenID Connect for secure and delegated authentication.

Authorization: Enforce proper authorization controls to ensure that authenticated users have appropriate access privileges. Implement role-based access control (RBAC) or attribute-based access control (ABAC) to manage user permissions effectively. Validate user roles and permissions before allowing access to sensitive resources.

Secure Communication: Ensure that the communication between clients and your API endpoints is secure. Use HTTPS/TLS to encrypt data in transit, preventing unauthorized interception and tampering. Enable strong encryption protocols and cipher suites, and configure secure server certificates to establish a trusted connection.

Input Validation and Sanitization: Validate and sanitize all user-supplied inputs to prevent injection attacks and other security vulnerabilities. Implement strict input validation checks to reject malicious or malformed data. Use whitelisting or parameterized queries to avoid code injection attacks such as SQL injection or cross-site scripting (XSS).

API Rate Limiting: Implement rate limiting mechanisms to prevent abuse, protect against brute-force attacks, and ensure fair usage of your API resources. Enforce limits on the number of requests per time interval, per user, or per API endpoint. Consider implementing techniques like token bucket or leaky bucket algorithms to manage request rates effectively.

Error Handling and Logging: Implement proper error handling and logging mechanisms to identify and respond to security incidents. Avoid disclosing sensitive information in error messages. Log relevant details such as request/response information, timestamps, and user identifiers to aid in security audits and incident investigations.

API Security Testing: Regularly conduct security testing and vulnerability assessments on your API endpoints. This can include techniques like penetration testing, vulnerability scanning, and code reviews. Identify and remediate any security weaknesses or vulnerabilities discovered during testing to strengthen your API's security posture.

Two-Factor Authentication (2FA): Consider implementing two-factor authentication to add an extra layer of security. 2FA requires users to provide a second form of authentication, such as a one-time password (OTP) generated by a mobile app or sent via SMS, in addition to their username and password.

Security Headers: Include appropriate security headers in your API responses to provide additional security controls. Common security headers include Content Security Policy (CSP), Strict-Transport-Security (HSTS), and X-XSS-Protection. These headers help prevent cross-site scripting, clickjacking, and other security attacks.

Regular Security Updates: Stay updated with security best practices and vulnerabilities related to your API framework, libraries, and dependencies. Regularly apply security patches and updates to protect against known vulnerabilities. Subscribe to security mailing lists and follow security advisories from relevant sources to stay informed about the latest security threats.

Secure Third-Party Integrations: Ensure that any third-party integrations used by your API follow secure coding practices and adhere to the necessary security standards. Validate the security practices of third-party providers, perform due diligence, and establish secure communication channels with them.

By implementing these security measures, you can significantly enhance the security and trustworthiness of your API endpoints, safeguarding sensitive data and providing a secure environment for your API consumers.

Rate limiting and throttling

Rate limiting and throttling are essential techniques for controlling and managing the rate of incoming requests to your API. They help prevent abuse, ensure fair usage of resources, and protect your API from performance degradation or denial of service attacks. Here are some key considerations for implementing rate limiting and throttling in your API:

Define Usage Policies: Establish clear usage policies that define the limits and restrictions for different types of API consumers. Consider factors such as the number of requests per time interval, the type of API operation, user roles, or subscription tiers. Clearly communicate these policies to API consumers through documentation or API response headers.

Determine Rate Limiting Strategy: Choose an appropriate rate limiting strategy based on your API's requirements and resources. Common strategies include:

- Fixed Window: Set a fixed number of requests allowed within a specific time window (e.g., 100 requests per minute).
- Sliding Window: Allow a certain number of requests per minute, but spread them evenly over smaller time intervals (e.g., 100 requests per minute, evenly distributed across seconds).
- Token Bucket: Assign tokens to users, where each request consumes a token. Once the tokens are exhausted, further requests are denied until tokens replenish.

Identify Rate Limiting Granularity: Determine the level of granularity at which rate limits are applied. You can apply rate limits per user, per API key, per IP address, or per client application. Granularity depends on factors such as the desired level of control and the type of API consumers.

Consider Burst or Spike Protection: Account for burst or spike protection to handle sudden traffic surges or legitimate high-volume requests. Allow for short-term increased rate limits or define burst limits that allow a higher number of requests before rate limits are enforced.

Graceful Error Responses: When a rate limit is exceeded, respond with appropriate HTTP status codes (e.g., 429 - Too Many Requests) and include information on the available rate limit, retry-after time, and any additional instructions. Provide clear error messages that help API consumers understand the reason for the rate limit.

Monitoring and Analytics: Implement monitoring and analytics to track API usage and rate limit violations. Monitor request volumes, success rates, and rate limit usage. Analyze this data to identify patterns, potential abuse, or the need for adjusting rate limits. Consider using tools or services that provide real-time analytics and reporting capabilities.

Throttling Strategies: Throttling involves limiting the rate of requests to prevent overload or maintain system stability. It differs from rate limiting in that it applies to individual users or clients, whereas rate limiting is often applied globally. Implement throttling mechanisms, such as limiting the number of concurrent connections or the maximum requests per second, to ensure fair usage and prevent resource exhaustion.

Flexible Configuration: Design your rate limiting and throttling mechanisms to be configurable, allowing you to adjust limits dynamically based on the evolving needs of your API and its consumers. Consider providing API consumers with the ability to increase their rate limits by subscribing to higher tiers or obtaining special access tokens.

Caching Responses: Implement response caching to reduce the load on your API servers and improve performance. Cache responses for requests that are identical or fall within a certain time frame, allowing subsequent identical requests to be served from the cache without hitting the rate limits.

Communication and Documentation: Clearly communicate the rate limiting and throttling policies to your API consumers. Include the rate limit headers in API responses (e.g., X-RateLimit-Limit, X-RateLimit-Remaining) to provide transparency. Document the rate limits, throttling rules, and any applicable guidelines or recommendations to help API consumers understand and adhere to the restrictions.

By implementing effective rate limiting and throttling strategies, you can ensure fair usage of your API resources, protect your system from abuse, maintain performance stability, and provide a positive experience for your API consumers.

Chapter 10: Working with API Libraries and Frameworks

Introduction to API libraries in different programming languages

When working with APIs, using programming language-specific libraries can greatly simplify the process of making API requests and handling responses. These libraries provide a higher-level abstraction, encapsulating the complexities of HTTP communication, authentication, data serialization, and error handling. Here's an introduction to some commonly used API libraries in different programming languages:

Python: Requests

Requests is a popular library for making HTTP requests in Python. It provides a simple and intuitive API for sending HTTP GET, POST, PUT, and DELETE requests. It supports various authentication methods, handles cookies and sessions, and offers convenient features like automatic JSON decoding.

JavaScript: Axios

Axios is a widely used library for making HTTP requests in JavaScript, commonly used in both browser-based and Node.js applications. It offers a clean and easy-to-use API, supports promises, and provides features such as request cancellation, request interceptors, and automatic JSON parsing.

Java: OkHttp

OkHttp is a powerful HTTP client library for Java applications. It offers a concise and expressive API, supports HTTP/2 and SPDY, handles connection pooling, and provides advanced features like transparent response caching, cookie management, and streaming request/response bodies.

Ruby: RestClient

RestClient is a user-friendly HTTP client library for Ruby. It allows you to easily send GET, POST, PUT, and DELETE requests, handle different authentication methods, and process JSON and XML responses. It offers a simple interface and supports SSL/TLS encryption.

PHP: Guzzle

Guzzle is a versatile HTTP client library for PHP. It provides an intuitive API for making HTTP requests, supports various authentication methods, and handles features like cookies, redirects, and streaming responses. Guzzle also offers advanced features such as request middleware and concurrent requests.

C#: HttpClient

HttpClient is a powerful library for making HTTP requests in C#/.NET applications. It offers a modern and flexible API, supports async/await patterns for asynchronous programming, and provides features like automatic decompression, cookie handling, and request/response message customization.

Go: net/http package

Go's standard library includes the net/http package, which provides a comprehensive set of tools for working with HTTP. It offers a robust and efficient API for sending requests, handling responses, and managing cookies. It also supports features like timeouts, redirects, and request/response body streaming.

Node.js: node-fetch

node-fetch is a popular library for making HTTP requests in Node.js applications. It offers a simple and straightforward API, supports promises, and provides features like request/response headers manipulation, handling redirects, and automatic JSON parsing.

Swift: URLSession

URLSession is a built-in framework in Swift for making network requests. It provides a comprehensive set of tools for creating and managing URLSessionTasks, handling authentication, and processing JSON and other response formats. It supports both synchronous and asynchronous request execution.

Kotlin: Fuel

Fuel is a lightweight HTTP networking library for Kotlin. It offers a concise and expressive API for making HTTP requests, supports various authentication methods, and provides features like automatic serialization/deserialization of request/response bodies and progress tracking.

These are just a few examples of API libraries available in different programming languages. Using these libraries can significantly simplify the process of interacting with APIs, abstracting away low-level networking details and allowing developers to focus on application logic. Make sure to consult the official documentation and community resources for each library to learn more about their features, usage, and best practices.

Popular API frameworks and their features

API frameworks provide a structured and efficient way to build and deploy APIs, offering a range of features to simplify development, improve productivity, and enhance the performance of your API. Here's an introduction to some popular API frameworks and their key features:

Express.js (Node.js):

Express.js is a lightweight and flexible framework for building web APIs with Node.js. It offers a minimalistic and unopinionated approach, allowing developers to create APIs quickly and easily. Express.js provides features like routing, middleware support, request/response handling, and integration with various templating engines.

Django REST Framework (Python):

Django REST Framework is a powerful and popular framework for building RESTful APIs with Python and Django. It provides a comprehensive set of tools for API development, including automatic serialization, authentication and authorization, request/response parsing, and support for various data formats. It also offers features like throttling, pagination, and filtering.

Ruby on Rails (Ruby):

Ruby on Rails, often referred to as Rails, is a full-stack web development framework that includes robust support for building APIs. It follows the convention-over-configuration principle, providing features like routing, data modeling with ActiveRecord, request/response handling, authentication, and support for multiple response formats.

ASP.NET Core (C#):

ASP.NET Core is a cross-platform framework for building modern web APIs with C#. It offers a high-performance and modular architecture, supporting features like routing, middleware pipeline, model binding, authentication and authorization, content negotiation, and response caching. It also integrates well with other .NET technologies.

Laravel (PHP):

Laravel is a popular PHP framework that offers an elegant and expressive syntax for building web APIs. It provides a rich set of features, including routing, middleware support, request/response handling, authentication and authorization, caching, and database integration using the powerful ORM, Eloquent.

Flask (Python):

Flask is a lightweight and flexible framework for building APIs with Python. It follows a microframework approach, allowing developers to choose and integrate the desired components. Flask provides features like routing, request/response handling, error handling, and support for various extensions to add functionality as needed.

Spring Boot (Java):

Spring Boot is a widely used Java framework that simplifies the development of web APIs. It offers a convention-over-configuration approach, allowing developers to quickly set up and configure APIs. Spring Boot provides features like routing with Spring MVC, request/response handling, data validation, security, and seamless integration with other Spring modules.

Phoenix (Elixir):

Phoenix is a high-performance web framework built with Elixir, a functional programming language. It provides features like routing, request/response handling, WebSocket support, authentication, and support for real-time applications. Phoenix leverages the power of Elixir's concurrency model to handle high loads efficiently.

NestJS (Node.js):

NestJS is a progressive Node.js framework for building scalable and maintainable APIs. It combines elements of object-oriented programming, functional programming, and TypeScript to provide a robust and modular architecture. NestJS offers features like decorators-based routing, dependency injection, middleware support, validation, and GraphQL integration.

Play Framework (Java and Scala):

Play Framework is a high-productivity web framework for Java and Scala. It follows a reactive and non-blocking architecture, making it suitable for building highly scalable APIs. Play Framework provides features like routing, request/response handling, asynchronous programming, WebSocket support, and seamless integration with Akka.

These are just a few examples of popular API frameworks available for different programming languages. Each framework offers unique features, architectural patterns, and development paradigms. Consider the specific requirements of your project, the ecosystem and community support around the framework, and your familiarity with the programming language when choosing the right API framework for your needs.

Consuming APIs using client libraries

When working with APIs, client libraries provide a convenient way to interact with API endpoints and handle the underlying communication details. These libraries encapsulate the complexities of making HTTP requests, handling responses, and parsing data, allowing developers to focus on consuming and utilizing the API data efficiently. Here's an introduction to consuming APIs using client libraries in different programming languages:

Python: Requests

Requests is a popular library for making HTTP requests in Python. It simplifies the process of consuming APIs by providing a high-level interface that supports common HTTP methods like GET, POST, PUT, and DELETE. Requests handles authentication, headers, query parameters, and response parsing, making it easy to retrieve and work with API data.

JavaScript: Axios

Axios is a widely used HTTP client library in JavaScript for both browser-based and Node.js applications. It offers a clean and intuitive API for making HTTP requests, supporting features like sending query parameters, setting headers, handling request and response interceptors, and automatically parsing JSON data.

Java: Retrofit

Retrofit is a popular HTTP client library in Java that simplifies API consumption. It provides a declarative and type-safe API for defining the API endpoints, handling request serialization, and parsing response data. Retrofit supports various data formats, authentication methods, and customizable request headers.

Ruby: RestClient

RestClient is a user-friendly HTTP client library in Ruby that simplifies API consumption. It offers a simple and intuitive API for making HTTP requests, handling authentication, setting headers, and parsing response data. RestClient supports multiple data formats like JSON, XML, and form data.

PHP: Guzzle

Guzzle is a powerful HTTP client library in PHP that provides a flexible and feature-rich API for consuming APIs. It supports various HTTP methods, query parameters, headers, authentication methods, and response parsing. Guzzle also offers features like request middleware, concurrent requests, and streaming responses.

C#: HttpClient

HttpClient is a built-in class in the .NET framework that simplifies API consumption in C#. It provides a straightforward API for making HTTP requests, setting headers, handling query parameters, and parsing response data. HttpClient supports async/await patterns, allowing for efficient and non-blocking API interactions.

Go: net/http package

Go's standard library includes the net/http package, which provides a complete set of tools for consuming APIs. It offers functions for making HTTP requests, setting headers, handling query parameters, and parsing response data. The net/http package supports concurrency and provides efficient methods for working with API endpoints.

Swift: URLSession

URLSession is a built-in framework in Swift that simplifies API consumption. It offers a comprehensive set of tools for making HTTP requests, handling headers and query parameters, and parsing response data. URLSession supports both synchronous and asynchronous requests, making it suitable for different scenarios.

Kotlin: Fuel

Fuel is a lightweight HTTP client library for Kotlin that simplifies API consumption. It provides a concise and expressive API for making HTTP requests, handling query parameters, headers, and authentication. Fuel also supports automatic serialization and deserialization of request and response bodies.

Node.js: node-fetch

node-fetch is a widely used library in Node.js for making HTTP requests and consuming APIs. It offers a simple and intuitive API similar to the browser's fetch API. It supports common HTTP methods, headers, query parameters, and response parsing, making it easy to consume APIs in Node.js applications.

These client libraries provide a streamlined approach to consuming APIs by abstracting away the complexities of HTTP communication, authentication, and response handling. They offer a range of features and flexibility, allowing developers to efficiently retrieve and process data from APIs in their preferred programming language. Make sure to refer to the documentation and community resources of each library for detailed usage instructions and best practices.

Chapter 11: Advanced API Concepts

Pagination and result filtering

When working with APIs that return large amounts of data, it's common to implement pagination and result filtering mechanisms to retrieve and manage data more efficiently. Pagination allows you to retrieve data in chunks or pages, while result filtering enables you to narrow down the data based on specific criteria. Here's an introduction to pagination and result filtering in API consumption:

Pagination:

Pagination is the process of dividing a large dataset into smaller, manageable chunks or pages. It helps reduce the amount of data retrieved in a single API request, improving performance and resource utilization. Common pagination techniques include:

- Offset-based pagination: The API response includes a parameter specifying the number of results to skip and the maximum number of results to return in each page.
- Cursor-based pagination: The API response includes a cursor or token that represents a

specific position in the dataset. The cursor is used to retrieve the next set of results.

- Page-based pagination: The API response includes a page number and a fixed number of results per page. It allows you to navigate through the dataset by requesting specific pages.

Implementing pagination involves passing appropriate parameters in API requests to specify the desired page size, current page, or cursor position. The API server then responds with the relevant subset of data, along with additional metadata such as total count or next/previous page information.

Result Filtering:

Result filtering allows you to retrieve a subset of data that matches specific criteria or conditions. Filtering can be based on various factors such as query parameters, headers, or request payloads. Some common filtering techniques include:

- Query parameters: API endpoints may accept query parameters that define filter conditions. For example, filtering by date range, category, or specific attributes.
- Field selection: APIs often provide the ability to specify the desired fields to be included or excluded in the API response. This helps reduce unnecessary data transfer.

- Sorting: APIs may allow you to sort the results based on specific fields, such as ascending or descending order.

By applying appropriate filters, you can reduce the response payload size, minimize network traffic, and retrieve only the data that meets your requirements.

When consuming APIs with pagination and result filtering, it's important to understand the specific pagination and filtering mechanisms supported by the API you're working with. The API documentation will provide details on the available parameters, their usage, and the structure of the API responses when pagination and filtering are applied.

It's also worth noting that pagination and filtering often work in conjunction, allowing you to navigate through large datasets while refining the results based on specific criteria. By effectively using pagination and result filtering, you can optimize your API consumption, improve performance, and obtain the desired subset of data efficiently.

Asynchronous and batch processing

Asynchronous and batch processing techniques are essential when working with APIs that involve time-consuming or resource-intensive operations. These techniques optimize performance, improve efficiency, and enable the processing of large volumes of data. Here's an introduction to asynchronous and batch processing in API consumption:

Asynchronous Processing:

Asynchronous processing allows you to execute API requests without blocking the execution flow of your application. Instead of waiting for each API request to complete before moving on to the next one, asynchronous processing enables parallel or concurrent execution of multiple requests. This can significantly improve the overall performance and responsiveness of your application. Common techniques for asynchronous processing include:

- Callbacks: Using callbacks, you can provide a function to be executed when an API request completes. This allows you to continue with other tasks while waiting for the response.

- Promises: Promises provide a more structured and readable way to handle asynchronous operations. They allow you to chain operations and handle success or failure cases.
- Async/await: Async/await is a modern approach that simplifies asynchronous programming by using async functions and the await keyword. It allows you to write asynchronous code that looks similar to synchronous code, improving readability.

By leveraging asynchronous processing, you can initiate multiple API requests simultaneously, handle responses as they become available, and maximize the utilization of system resources.

Batch Processing:

Batch processing involves sending a group of API requests as a single batch or collection. This is particularly useful when you need to perform a set of related operations or when making multiple requests for the same resource. Batch processing offers benefits such as reduced network overhead and improved efficiency. Common techniques for batch processing include:

- Batch API Endpoints: Some APIs provide special endpoints specifically designed for handling batches of requests. These endpoints accept an array or collection of requests as input and process them in a single operation.

- Queueing Systems: Queueing systems like RabbitMQ, Apache Kafka, or AWS Simple Queue Service (SQS) allow you to enqueue API requests and process them in a batch-oriented manner. These systems provide reliable and scalable mechanisms for handling large volumes of requests.

Batch processing allows you to optimize API interactions by combining multiple requests into a single operation, minimizing the overhead associated with individual requests and reducing network latency.

When implementing asynchronous and batch processing in API consumption, it's important to consider the specific requirements of your application and the capabilities provided by the API you're working with. Not all APIs support asynchronous or batch processing, so consult the API documentation to understand the recommended approaches and limitations.

By effectively utilizing asynchronous processing and batch operations, you can enhance the performance, scalability, and efficiency of your API consumption, particularly when dealing with time-consuming or resource-intensive tasks.

Webhooks and event-driven APIs

Webhooks and event-driven APIs are powerful mechanisms for real-time communication and enabling reactive systems. They allow applications to receive notifications and data updates from external systems, triggering actions or processing data based on specific events. Here's an introduction to webhooks and event-driven APIs:

Webhooks:

Webhooks are a way for applications to receive real-time notifications or callbacks from external systems. Instead of constantly polling or repeatedly making API requests to check for updates, the external system sends an HTTP request to a specified URL (the webhook endpoint) when a relevant event occurs. The application can then process the received data or trigger a specific action. Key points about webhooks include:

- Setup: To use webhooks, you need to provide a callback URL to the external system. This URL should be accessible to receive incoming HTTP requests.
- Event Payload: The payload of the webhook request typically contains information about

the event that occurred, including relevant data or metadata.

- Authentication and Security: Webhooks may use mechanisms like signatures or tokens to ensure the authenticity and integrity of the incoming requests.
- Response Handling: Applications should respond to the webhook requests with an appropriate HTTP status code to confirm receipt or provide necessary feedback.

Webhooks enable real-time communication between systems and allow applications to respond promptly to events without the need for constant polling.

Event-Driven APIs:

Event-driven APIs provide a more structured and scalable approach to building systems that rely on real-time communication and event notifications. Instead of relying solely on webhooks, event-driven APIs are designed to publish and consume events using a publish-subscribe pattern. Key concepts related to event-driven APIs include:

- Event Publishers: Applications or systems that generate and publish events to a centralized event broker or message queue.
- Event Consumers: Applications or systems that subscribe to specific events and react accordingly when those events occur.

- Event Schema and Payload: Events have a well-defined schema and contain relevant data or metadata to convey the information associated with the event.
- Event Brokers or Message Queues: These are the central components that facilitate the reliable distribution of events to the subscribed consumers.

Event-driven APIs enable loosely coupled architectures, allowing different components or systems to react independently to specific events while promoting scalability and flexibility.

Implementing webhooks and event-driven APIs requires understanding the event types, their associated data structures, and the communication protocols supported by the external systems or API providers. Additionally, you need to ensure the reliability, security, and error handling mechanisms in your application to handle webhook requests or process events effectively.

By leveraging webhooks and event-driven APIs, applications can build real-time and reactive systems, enabling timely notifications, data updates, and seamless integration with external systems.

Chapter 12: Future of APIs

Emerging trends in APIs

The world of APIs is constantly evolving, driven by technological advancements and changing industry needs. Staying updated with emerging trends is crucial for developers and organizations to leverage the latest capabilities and deliver innovative solutions. Here are some prominent emerging trends in the API landscape:

GraphQL:

GraphQL is an open-source query language for APIs that enables clients to request and retrieve specific data requirements from the server. It provides a flexible and efficient way to retrieve only the data needed, reducing over-fetching and under-fetching of data. GraphQL's ability to aggregate data from multiple sources and its introspection capabilities make it increasingly popular for building efficient and client-driven APIs.

Serverless Architectures:

Serverless architectures, also known as Function as a Service (FaaS), are gaining traction in the API world. Serverless platforms, such as AWS Lambda, Azure Functions, and Google Cloud Functions, allow developers to focus on writing code for specific functionalities without managing the underlying infrastructure. APIs can be built and deployed as individual functions, scaling automatically based on demand, and providing cost-effective solutions for handling API workloads.

Event-Driven Architectures:

Event-driven architectures, where systems communicate and react to events, are becoming more prevalent in API development. Event-driven APIs allow for asynchronous and decoupled communication between components, enabling systems to react in real-time to events and trigger actions. This approach supports scalability, responsiveness, and flexibility, particularly in scenarios involving microservices, IoT, and real-time data processing.

AI-powered APIs:

With the advancements in Artificial Intelligence (AI) and Machine Learning (ML), AI-powered APIs are becoming increasingly popular. These APIs provide pre-built models and capabilities that enable developers to integrate AI functionalities into their applications without requiring deep expertise in AI/ML. AI-powered APIs can handle tasks like natural language processing, image recognition, sentiment analysis, and recommendation systems, empowering developers to build intelligent and data-driven applications quickly.

API Marketplaces:

API marketplaces are platforms that facilitate the discovery, consumption, and monetization of APIs. They provide a centralized hub where developers can explore and access a wide range of APIs offered by different providers. API marketplaces enable organizations to showcase and distribute their APIs to a broader audience, fostering innovation, collaboration, and API ecosystem growth.

Hypermedia APIs:

Hypermedia APIs, based on the principles of Hypermedia as the Engine of Application State (HATEOAS), aim to improve API discoverability, interoperability, and flexibility. These APIs include links and metadata in their responses, allowing clients to navigate and interact with related resources dynamically. Hypermedia APIs enable clients to evolve and adapt to changes in the API without relying on prior knowledge of resource URIs, promoting loose coupling and enhancing API usability.

Low-Code and No-Code APIs:

Low-code and no-code development platforms are gaining popularity, allowing non-technical users to build applications and integrations without writing extensive code. APIs play a significant role in these platforms, enabling users to connect with external systems, services, and data sources through pre-built API integrations. Low-code and no-code APIs simplify the integration process and empower citizen developers to create applications with reduced development effort.

Keeping an eye on these emerging trends can help developers and organizations make informed decisions when designing, developing, and consuming APIs. Understanding and adopting these trends can lead to more efficient, scalable, and innovative solutions that leverage the latest advancements in the API landscape.

GraphQL and its advantages

GraphQL is an open-source query language for APIs that has gained significant popularity in recent years. It offers a modern and efficient approach to fetching and manipulating data, providing several advantages over traditional RESTful APIs. Here's an introduction to GraphQL and its key advantages:

Declarative Data Fetching:

One of the primary advantages of GraphQL is its declarative nature. With GraphQL, clients can specify exactly what data they need and the structure of the response using a GraphQL query. This eliminates the problem of over-fetching or under-fetching data commonly associated with REST APIs, where predefined endpoints may return more or less data than required. GraphQL ensures that clients receive precisely the data they request, reducing network overhead and improving performance.

Efficient Data Retrieval:

GraphQL allows clients to retrieve multiple resources and their related data in a single request. With GraphQL's ability to specify nested fields and relationships in a query, clients can fetch all the required data in a hierarchical manner. This eliminates the need for multiple API requests to retrieve related resources and reduces the problem of "N+1" queries often encountered in REST APIs. GraphQL optimizes data retrieval by minimizing round trips and reducing the amount of data transferred over the network.

Strongly Typed Schema:

GraphQL uses a strongly typed schema to define the API's capabilities and data model. The schema acts as a contract between the server and the client, specifying the available types, fields, and operations. This schema-driven approach provides several benefits, including:

- Self-Documentation: The GraphQL schema serves as a comprehensive and self-documenting resource that describes the API's capabilities and data structures. Clients can explore and understand the API using introspection and easily discover available fields, relationships, and their types.
- Type Safety: By enforcing a strict schema, GraphQL provides type safety and validation at the API level. It ensures that clients send valid queries and receive well-structured responses, reducing the chances of runtime errors.
- Schema Evolution: GraphQL's schema-first approach allows for easy schema evolution and versioning. New fields and types can be added without breaking existing clients, and deprecated fields can be phased out gradually. This flexibility simplifies API evolution and ensures backward compatibility.

Reduced Overfetching and Underfetching:

Over-fetching and under-fetching of data are common challenges in traditional REST APIs, where predefined endpoints return fixed data structures. This often leads to unnecessary data transfer or insufficient data retrieval. GraphQL solves this problem by allowing clients to precisely specify the required fields and relationships in a query. Clients receive only the data they need, eliminating over-fetching and under-fetching scenarios and improving efficiency.

Rapid Iteration and Development:

GraphQL enables rapid iteration and development cycles by empowering front-end developers to query and retrieve data as per their requirements. With GraphQL's flexibility, clients can request new fields or data structures without requiring changes to the server's API endpoints. This decoupling of the client and server allows both teams to work independently, iterate quickly, and deliver features more efficiently.

Ecosystem and Tooling:

GraphQL has a vibrant ecosystem with various tools, libraries, and frameworks that simplify its adoption and implementation. These tools offer features such as schema generation, query validation, documentation generation, and client code generation. Popular tools like Apollo GraphQL, Relay, and GraphiQL provide powerful development and debugging capabilities, enhancing the overall GraphQL development experience.

By leveraging GraphQL's declarative data fetching, efficient data retrieval, strongly typed schema, and reduced over-fetching/under-fetching, developers can create more performant and flexible APIs. The GraphQL ecosystem's tooling and rapid development cycles further contribute to its popularity and widespread adoption across different domains and platforms.

Serverless APIs and microservices

Serverless computing and microservices architectures have revolutionized the way APIs are designed, deployed, and managed. They offer numerous benefits in terms of scalability, cost-efficiency, and flexibility. Let's explore serverless APIs and microservices in more detail:

Serverless Computing:

Serverless computing, also known as Function as a Service (FaaS), abstracts away the infrastructure management, allowing developers to focus solely on writing code for specific functionalities or business logic. In a serverless environment, APIs are implemented as individual functions or microservices that are deployed and executed in response to specific events or HTTP requests. Key advantages of serverless computing include:

- Auto-scaling: Serverless platforms automatically scale the execution of functions based on incoming requests or event triggers. This ensures optimal resource allocation and eliminates the need for manual capacity planning.
- Cost Efficiency: With serverless, you pay only for the actual execution time of functions, rather than for provisioning and maintaining dedicated servers. This pay-per-use model offers cost savings, especially for applications with variable or unpredictable workloads.
- Rapid Development: Serverless environments provide simplified deployment and configuration processes, allowing developers to focus on writing business logic. This facilitates faster development cycles and promotes agility.

Microservices Architecture:

Microservices architecture involves breaking down large monolithic applications into smaller, independent services that can be developed, deployed, and scaled individually. Microservices communicate with each other via APIs, often using lightweight protocols like HTTP/REST or messaging systems. Key benefits of microservices include:

- Scalability: Microservices can be independently scaled based on their specific resource requirements, allowing for efficient resource utilization. This enables systems to handle varying workloads and achieve higher scalability.
- Loose Coupling: Each microservice has a well-defined boundary and can be developed, deployed, and updated independently. This loose coupling ensures that changes in one microservice do not impact others, promoting agility and enabling faster iterations.
- Fault Isolation: Microservices operate as separate entities, which means that failures or issues in one microservice do not bring down the entire system. This promotes fault isolation and enhances the overall robustness of the application.

Serverless APIs and Microservices:

Serverless computing and microservices are often used together to build highly scalable and resilient APIs. In this context, serverless APIs are implemented as individual functions or microservices, which can be orchestrated and interconnected to form a complete API system. Advantages of serverless APIs and microservices include:

- Granular Scaling: With serverless APIs, each function or microservice can be scaled independently based on its specific usage patterns and resource demands. This granular scaling allows efficient resource allocation and cost optimization.
- Flexibility and Agility: Serverless APIs and microservices enable teams to work on different services independently, promoting agile development and facilitating rapid iterations. This flexibility is particularly useful in environments where different teams or third-party providers contribute to the overall API ecosystem.
- Fault Tolerance and Resilience: The distributed nature of microservices and serverless architectures enhances fault tolerance and resilience. If a particular function or microservice fails, other parts of the API system can continue to function, reducing the impact on overall availability.
- Seamless Integration: Microservices and serverless APIs can integrate with various

external systems and services, enabling organizations to leverage existing infrastructure or third-party capabilities. This integration capability facilitates building comprehensive and feature-rich API ecosystems.

Serverless APIs and microservices offer a scalable, cost-efficient, and flexible approach to building APIs that can adapt to changing business requirements. By leveraging serverless computing and microservices architecture, organizations can achieve higher scalability, reduce infrastructure costs, and promote agility in API development and management.

Printed in Great Britain
by Amazon